STEWS

STEWS

a collection of recipes for delicious meals

LOVE FOOD™

Cover by Talking Design
Design concept by Fiona Roberts
Produced by the Bridgewater Book Company Ltd
New photography: David Jordan
Home economist: Jacqueline Bellefontaine

Notes for the Reader

This book uses imperial, metric, or US cup measurements. Follow the same units of measurement throughout; do not mix imperial and metric. All spoon measurements are level: teaspoons are assumed to be 5 ml, and tablespoons are assumed to be 15 ml. Unless otherwise stated, milk is assumed to be whole, eggs and individual vegetables such as potatoes are medium, and pepper is freshly ground black pepper. Recipes using raw or very lightly cooked eggs should be avoided by infants, the elderly, pregnant women, convalescents, and anyone suffering from an illness.

Introduction

Stews are the perfect food for when the temperature has dipped outside and it is cold, wet, and blustery, or if you simply want a little wholesome comfort food and nothing else will do. This is what this book is all about—hearty, filling, satisfying, and warming meals for all tastes and appetites. Stewing is ideal for long, slow cooking. Stews are cooked on the stove, and the heat needs to be gentle so that the liquid is left to simmer rather than boil, and this can take some fine-tuning. This book also includes some classic casseroles. They are very similar to stews, but they are cooked in the oven, not on the stove, and normally have slightly less liquid.

For cooking stews, choose a large, heavy-bottom pan—one that will withstand long, steady cooking without the bottom burning or buckling, or the food sticking to the bottom. It should have a tight-fitting lid so that the liquid does not evaporate during cooking. Casseroles require a casserole dish that is both flameproof and ovenproof and has a tight-fitting lid.

When preparing your stew, it is important that any meat is browned and sealed before slow cooking commences. This ensures that the color, and most importantly the flavor, is preserved rather than leeching out into the liquid. There should be just enough meat to cover the bottom of the pan or skillet—more could mean uneven sealing and both the flavor and appearance of the dish will be spoiled. If there is too much meat to seal in one go, then work in two or three batches.

Many of these recipes require a bouquet garni. To make one, take 2 pieces of celery stalk, each about 3 inches/7.5 cm long. Lay a good selection of herbs on the inside of one of the celery pieces and place the other on top. Secure firmly with fine kitchen string. Choose from fresh or dried bay leaves and fresh thyme, oregano, parsley, tarragon, mint, and chervil sprigs.

Whichever recipe you choose to make from this heart-warming collection, you are sure to be delighted with the result and will want to cook it again and again, as well as all the other great dishes on offer.

For a dish to be successful, you need to start with the right ingredients, of good quality. In the case of meat, it is particularly important that the appropriate cut of meat is used for the cooking method involved. Very lean, fine-grain meat is best cooked quickly by being broiled, grilled, or fried, whereas coarser cuts, or those with in-built reserves of fat, are ideal for being cooked gently over time in a stew or casserole, resulting in a meltingly tender, fully flavored result. Slow-cooking is a method that enables the meat flavors to meld with those of the accompanying vegetables, fruit, herbs, and spices in the pot. All you have to do the night before is chop up some meat and vegetables, and the next morning toss them in the slow cooker and switch it on. Food retains its moisture well, and is evenly and gently distributed around the sides as well as the bottom of the pot.

MEAT PERFECTION

The recipes in this chapter offer you the opportunity to sample all kinds of delicious combinations, from the simple and hearty to the fruity and fiery. For instance, in Pork Oriental, chunks of pork are teamed with tangy pineapple for a sweet-and-sour taste experience, while Mediterranean Lamb with Apricots and Pistachios features the warmly spiced mellow fruitiness of North African cuisine. Or choose from Thick Beef and Pearl Onion Casserole, laced with full-bodied red wine with a touch of zesty orange, or Pepper Pot-Style Stew, another beef and vegetable dish, this time with squash, okra, and tomatoes, plus a kick of green chili as well as hot pepper sauce. Such variety means that you'll be sure to find a stew or casserole to match your mood, the season, or occasion.

SERVES 6

2 tbsp olive oil

1 lb/450 g pearl onions, peeled but kept whole (see below)

2 garlic cloves, halved

2 lb/900 g stewing beef, cubed

½ tsp ground cinnamon

1 tsp ground cloves

1 tsp ground cumin

2 tbsp tomato paste

generous 3 cups full-bodied red wine

grated rind and juice of 1 orange

1 bay leaf

salt and pepper

1 tbsp chopped fresh flat-leaf parsley, to garnish

boiled or mashed potatoes, to serve

Thick Beef and Pearl Onion Casserole

If you find it difficult to peel the pearl onions, bring a large pan of water to a boil, then remove from the heat and plunge the onions quickly into the hot water. Remove and plunge into cold water before peeling.

• Preheat the oven to 300°F/150°C. Heat the oil in a large, flameproof casserole and cook the whole onions and garlic, stirring frequently, for 5 minutes, or until softened and beginning to brown. Add the beef and cook over high heat, stirring frequently, for 5 minutes, or until browned on all sides and sealed.

• Stir the spices and tomato paste into the casserole and add salt and pepper to taste. Pour in the wine, scraping any sediment from the bottom of the casserole, then add the orange rind and juice and the bay leaf. Bring to a boil and cover.

• Cook in the preheated oven for about 1¼ hours. Remove the lid and cook the casserole for an additional hour, stirring once or twice, until the meat is tender. Remove from the oven and garnish with the parsley. Serve hot, accompanied by boiled or mashed potatoes.

SERVES 4

1 lb/450 g braising beef steak

1½ tbsp all-purpose flour

1 tsp hot paprika

1–1½ tsp chili powder

1 tsp ground ginger

2 tbsp olive oil

1 large onion, cut into chunks

3 garlic cloves, sliced

2 celery stalks, sliced

8 oz/225 g carrots, chopped

1¼ cups lager

1¼ cups beef stock

12 oz/350 g potatoes, chopped

1 red bell pepper, seeded and chopped

2 corncobs, halved

4 oz/115 g tomatoes, cut into fourths

1 cup shelled fresh or frozen peas

1 tbsp chopped fresh cilantro

salt and pepper

Beef and Vegetable Stew with Corn

If fresh corncob is unavailable, use 4 oz/115 g baby corn, halved lengthwise, or canned, drained corn kernels, and add to the stew with the tomatoes and peas.

• Trim any fat or gristle from the beef and cut into 1-inch/2.5-cm chunks. Mix the flour and spices together. Toss the beef in the spiced flour until well coated.

• Heat the oil in a large, heavy-bottom pan and cook the onion, garlic, and celery, stirring frequently, for 5 minutes, or until softened. Add the beef and cook over high heat, stirring frequently, for 3 minutes, or until browned on all sides and sealed.

• Add the carrots, then remove from the heat. Gradually stir in the lager and stock, then return to the heat and bring to a boil, stirring. Reduce the heat, then cover and simmer, stirring occasionally, for 1½ hours.

• Add the potatoes to the pan and simmer for an additional 15 minutes. Add the red bell pepper and corncobs and simmer for 15 minutes, then add the tomatoes and peas and simmer for an additional 10 minutes, or until the beef and vegetables are tender. Season to taste with salt and pepper, then stir in the cilantro and serve.

SERVES 4–6

2 lb/900 g stewing beef, such as chuck or leg
2 onions, thinly sliced
2 carrots, thickly sliced
4 large garlic cloves, bruised but kept whole
1 large fresh bouquet garni
4 juniper berries
generous 2 cups full-bodied dry red wine, such as Fitou
2 tbsp brandy
2 tbsp olive oil
8 oz/225 g boned belly of pork, rind removed
1⅓ cups all-purpose flour
2 x 4-inch/10-cm strips of orange rind
½ cup black olives, pitted and rinsed
beef stock, if needed
6 tbsp water
salt and pepper

TO GARNISH

1 tbsp chopped fresh flat-leaf parsley
finely grated orange rind

Beef Stew with Olives

This traditional Provençal dish is often served with buttered noodles, but a mound of hot mashed potatoes also makes an ideal accompaniment. For a two-course meal in a pot Provençal-style, serve the flavorsome juices in a soup bowl with the noodles as a first course, then the meat and vegetables as a second course. You could also substitute 4½ oz/125 g unsmoked lardons for the belly of pork.

- Trim the beef and cut it into 2-inch/5-cm chunks, then put the beef in a large glass or earthenware bowl and add the onions, carrots, garlic, bouquet garni, juniper berries, and salt and pepper to taste. Pour over the wine, brandy, and oil and stir well. Cover with plastic wrap and let marinate in the refrigerator for 24 hours.
- Remove the beef and marinade from the refrigerator 30 minutes before you plan to cook and preheat the oven to 325°F/160°C. Meanwhile, cut the belly of pork into ¼-inch/5-mm strips. Bring a pan of water to a boil and add the pork. Return to the boil and blanch for 3 minutes, then drain and set aside.
- Using a slotted spoon, remove the beef from the marinade and pat dry with paper towels. Put the beef and 3 tablespoons of the flour, with salt and pepper to taste, in a plastic bag, then hold the top closed and shake until the beef chunks are lightly coated all over. Remove from the bag and shake off any excess flour, then set aside.
- Transfer half the pork slices to a 3.6-quart/3.4-liter flameproof casserole. Top with the beef and marinade, including the vegetables and bouquet garni, and add the orange rind and olives. Scatter the remaining pork slices over. Top up with stock to cover all the ingredients.
- Mix the remaining flour with the water to form a thick, pliable paste. Slowly bring the casserole to a boil on the stove, then put the lid on the casserole and use your fingers to press the paste around the sides to form a tight seal. Cook in the preheated oven for 1 hour. Reduce the oven temperature to 275°F/140°C and cook for an additional 3 hours.
- Remove the casserole from the oven and use a serrated knife to cut off the seal. Use the tip of the knife to ensure that the beef and carrots are tender. If not, re-cover the casserole and return it to the oven, testing again after 15 minutes.
- Using a large metal spoon, skim any fat from the surface and adjust the seasoning if necessary. Remove the bouquet garni, then sprinkle the parsley and orange rind over the top and serve. Alternatively, let cool completely, cover, and chill overnight. Before reheating, scrape the solid fat off the surface. Reheat, then garnish and serve.

SERVES 4

1 lb/450 g braising beef steak
1½ tbsp all-purpose flour
2 tbsp olive oil
1 red onion, chopped
3–4 garlic cloves, crushed
1 fresh green chili, seeded and chopped
3 celery stalks, sliced
4 whole cloves
1 tsp ground allspice
1–2 tsp hot pepper sauce, or to taste
2½ cups beef stock
8 oz/225 g seeded and peeled squash, such as acorn, cut into small chunks
1 large red bell pepper, seeded and chopped
4 tomatoes, coarsely chopped
4 oz/115 g okra, trimmed and halved
mixed wild and basmati rice, to serve

Pepper Pot-Style Stew

This spicy stew can be as hot or as mild as you like. If your taste is for fiery heat, add more of the hot pepper sauce, but if you find that your hand has slipped while adding it and that it is now too hot, stir in some mashed potatoes to help neutralize the heat.

• Trim any fat or gristle from the beef and cut into 1-inch/2.5-cm chunks. Toss the beef in the flour until well coated and reserve any remaining flour.

• Heat the oil in a large, heavy-bottom pan and cook the onion, garlic, chili, and celery with the cloves and allspice, stirring frequently, for 5 minutes, or until softened. Add the beef and cook over high heat, stirring frequently, for 3 minutes, or until browned on all sides and sealed. Sprinkle in the reserved flour and cook, stirring constantly, for 2 minutes, then remove from the heat.

• Add the hot pepper sauce and gradually stir in the stock, then return to the heat and bring to a boil, stirring. Reduce the heat, then cover and simmer, stirring occasionally, for 1½ hours.

• Add the squash and red bell pepper to the pan and simmer for an additional 15 minutes. Add the tomatoes and okra and simmer for an additional 15 minutes, or until the beef is tender. Serve with mixed wild and basmati rice.

SERVES 4–6

3/4 stick butter
2 tbsp corn oil
2/3 cup smoked lardons, blanched for 30 seconds, then drained and patted dry
2 lb/900 g stewing beef, such as chuck or leg
2 large garlic cloves, crushed
1 carrot, diced
1 leek, halved and sliced
1 onion, finely chopped
2 tbsp all-purpose flour
1½ cups full-bodied red Burgundy wine, such as Hermitage or Côtes du Rhône
about generous 2 cups beef stock
1 tbsp tomato paste
1 fresh bouquet garni
12 pickling onions, peeled but kept whole
12 white mushrooms
salt and pepper
chopped fresh flat-leaf parsley, to garnish
French bread, to serve

Beef Bourguignon

This casserole is customarily served with the same wine used in cooking. Like most meat casseroles, it tastes best made a day in advance and reheated. Remove from the oven after 1½ hours simmering. The next day, cook the mushrooms and onions, then add to the casserole and slowly bring to a boil on the stove. Cook in the preheated oven for 35-40 minutes, or until the beef is very tender.

• Preheat the oven to 300°F/150°C. Heat 2 tablespoons of the butter and 1 tablespoon of the oil in a large, flameproof casserole. Cook the lardons over medium-high heat, stirring, for 2 minutes, or until beginning to brown. Using a slotted spoon, remove from the casserole and drain on paper towels.

• Trim the beef and cut it into 2-inch/5-cm chunks. Add the beef to the casserole and cook over high heat, stirring frequently, for 5 minutes, or until browned on all sides and sealed, adding more of the butter or oil to the casserole as necessary. Using a slotted spoon, transfer the beef to a plate.

• Pour off all but 2 tablespoons of the fat from the casserole. Add the garlic, carrot, leek, and chopped onion and cook over medium heat, stirring frequently, for 3 minutes, or until the onion is beginning to soften. Sprinkle in the flour, and salt and pepper to taste, and cook, stirring constantly, for 2 minutes, then remove from the heat.

• Gradually stir in the wine and stock and add the tomato paste and bouquet garni, then return to the heat and bring to a boil, stirring and scraping any sediment from the bottom of the casserole.

• Return the beef and lardons to the casserole and add extra stock if necessary so that the ingredients are covered by about ½ inch/1 cm of liquid. Slowly return to a boil, then cover and cook in the preheated oven for 2 hours.

• Meanwhile, heat 2 tablespoons of the remaining butter and the remaining oil in a large sauté pan or skillet and cook the pickling onions over medium-high heat, stirring frequently, until golden all over. Using a slotted spoon, transfer the onions to a plate.

• Heat the remaining butter in the pan and cook the mushrooms, with salt and pepper to taste, stirring frequently, until golden brown. Remove from the pan and then stir them, with the onions, into the casserole. Re-cover and cook for an additional 30 minutes, or until the beef is very tender.

• Discard the bouquet garni, then adjust the seasoning to taste. Serve garnished with parsley, accompanied by plenty of French bread for mopping up all the juices.

SERVES 4

1 lb/450 g lean boneless lamb, such as leg of lamb or fillet
1½ tbsp all-purpose flour
1 tsp ground cloves
1–1½ tbsp olive oil
1 white onion, sliced
2–3 garlic cloves, sliced
1¼ cups orange juice
⅔ cup lamb stock or chicken stock
1 cinnamon stick, bruised
2 sweet (pointed, if available) red peppers, seeded and sliced into rings
4 tomatoes
salt and pepper
few fresh sprigs cilantro, plus 1 tbsp chopped fresh cilantro, to garnish

TO SERVE

mashed sweet potatoes mixed with chopped scallions
green vegetables

Lamb Stew with Sweet Red Bell Peppers

Sweet potatoes are very good for mashing and offer a tasty alternative to the traditional potato as an accompaniment. Try combining sweet potatoes with parsnips or carrot and mash together, then stir in a little chopped fresh cilantro.

- Preheat the oven to 375°F/190°C. Trim any fat or gristle from the lamb and cut into thin strips. Mix the flour and cloves together. Toss the lamb in the spiced flour until well coated and reserve any remaining spiced flour.
- Heat 1 tablespoon of the oil in a heavy-bottom skillet and cook the lamb over high heat, stirring frequently, for 3 minutes, or until browned on all sides and sealed. Using a slotted spoon, transfer to an ovenproof casserole.
- Add the onion and garlic to the skillet and cook over medium heat, stirring frequently, for 3 minutes, adding the extra oil if necessary. Sprinkle in the reserved spiced flour and cook, stirring constantly, for 2 minutes, then remove from the heat. Gradually stir in the orange juice and stock, then return to the heat and bring to a boil, stirring.
- Pour over the lamb in the casserole, then add the cinnamon stick, red bell peppers, tomatoes, and cilantro sprigs and stir well. Cover and cook in the preheated oven for 1½ hours, or until the lamb is tender.
- Discard the cinnamon stick, and adjust the seasoning to taste. Serve garnished with the chopped cilantro, accompanied by mashed sweet potatoes with scallions, and green vegetables.

SERVES 6

- 2 tbsp all-purpose flour
- 2 lb 4 oz/1 kg lean boneless lamb, cubed
- 2 tbsp olive oil
- 2 large onions, sliced
- 1 garlic clove, finely chopped
- 1¼ cups full-bodied red wine
- 2 tbsp red wine vinegar
- 14 oz/400 g canned chopped tomatoes
- generous ⅓ cup seedless raisins
- 1 tbsp ground cinnamon
- pinch of sugar
- 1 bay leaf
- salt and pepper
- paprika, to garnish

TOPPING

- ⅔ cup strained plain yogurt
- 2 garlic cloves, crushed
- salt and pepper

Cinnamon Lamb Casserole

Serve this dish with potatoes, rice, or a pilaf to soak up the delicious aromatic juices.

• Season the flour with pepper to taste and put it with the lamb in a plastic bag, then hold the top closed and shake until the lamb cubes are lightly coated all over. Remove the lamb from the bag, then shake off any excess flour and set aside.

• Heat the oil in a large, flameproof casserole and cook the onions and garlic, stirring frequently, for 5 minutes, or until softened. Add the lamb and cook over high heat, stirring frequently, for 5 minutes, or until browned on all sides and sealed.

• Stir the wine, vinegar, and tomatoes and their juice into the casserole, scraping any sediment from the bottom of the casserole, and bring to a boil. Reduce the heat and add the raisins, cinnamon, sugar, and bay leaf. Season to taste with salt and pepper. Cover and simmer gently for 2 hours, or until the lamb is tender.

• Meanwhile, make the topping. Put the yogurt into a small serving bowl, then stir in the garlic and season to taste with salt and pepper. Cover and chill in the refrigerator until required.

• Discard the bay leaf and serve the lamb hot, topped with a spoonful of the garlic yogurt and dusted with paprika.

SERVES 4

pinch of saffron threads
2 tbsp almost boiling water
1 lb/450 g lean boneless lamb, such as leg steaks
1½ tbsp all-purpose flour
1 tsp ground coriander
½ tsp ground cumin
½ tsp ground allspice
1 tbsp olive oil
1 onion, chopped
2–3 garlic cloves, chopped
scant 2 cups lamb or chicken stock
1 cinnamon stick, bruised
½ cup dried apricots, coarsely chopped
6 oz/175 g zucchini, sliced into half moons
4 oz/115 g cherry tomatoes
1 tbsp chopped fresh cilantro
salt and pepper
2 tbsp coarsely chopped pistachios, to garnish
couscous, to serve

Mediterranean Lamb with Apricots and Pistachios

Couscous is now available in an instant form, which is simply prepared: pour over boiling water and quickly stir, then cover and let stand for 5–8 minutes. Fluff up with a fork before serving. Alternatively, scatter a handful of raisins over the couscous and use boiling lamb, chicken, or vegetable stock in place of the water.

• Put the saffron threads in a heatproof pitcher with the water and let stand for at least 10 minutes to infuse. Trim off any fat or gristle from the lamb and cut into 1-inch/2.5-cm chunks. Mix the flour and spices together, then toss the lamb in the spiced flour until well coated and reserve any remaining spiced flour.

• Heat the oil in a large, heavy-bottom pan and cook the onion and garlic, stirring frequently, for 5 minutes, or until softened. Add the lamb and cook over high heat, stirring frequently, for 3 minutes, or until browned on all sides and sealed. Sprinkle in the reserved spiced flour and cook, stirring constantly, for 2 minutes, then remove from the heat.

• Gradually stir in the stock and the saffron and its soaking liquid, then return to the heat and bring to a boil, stirring. Add the cinnamon stick and apricots. Reduce the heat, then cover and simmer, stirring occasionally, for 1 hour.

• Add the zucchini and tomatoes and cook for an additional 15 minutes. Discard the cinnamon stick. Stir in the fresh cilantro and season to taste with salt and pepper. Serve sprinkled with the pistachios, accompanied by couscous.

Pork Oriental

SERVES 4

1 lb/450 g lean boneless pork
1½ tbsp all-purpose flour
1–2 tbsp olive oil
1 onion, cut into small wedges
2–3 garlic cloves, chopped
1-inch/2.5-cm piece fresh gingerroot, peeled and grated
1 tbsp tomato paste
1¼ cups chicken stock
8 oz/225 g canned pineapple chunks in natural juice
1–1½ tbsp dark soy sauce
1 red bell pepper, seeded and sliced
1 green bell pepper, seeded and sliced
1½ tbsp balsamic vinegar
4 scallions, diagonally sliced, to garnish

This dish also works well with chicken, turkey, or ham. Serve it with freshly cooked rice—stir in a little chopped fresh cilantro just before serving.

• Trim off any fat or gristle from the pork and cut into 1-inch/2.5-cm chunks. Toss the pork in the flour until well coated and reserve any remaining flour.

• Heat the oil in a large, heavy-bottom pan and cook the onion, garlic, and ginger, stirring frequently, for 5 minutes, or until softened. Add the pork and cook over high heat, stirring frequently, for 5 minutes, or until browned on all sides and sealed. Sprinkle in the reserved flour and cook, stirring constantly, for 2 minutes, then remove from the heat.

• Blend the tomato paste with the stock in a heatproof pitcher and gradually stir into the pan. Drain the pineapple, reserving both the fruit and juice, and stir the juice into the pan.

• Add the soy sauce to the pan, then return to the heat and bring to a boil, stirring. Reduce the heat, then cover and simmer, stirring occasionally, for 1 hour. Add the bell peppers and cook for an additional 15 minutes, or until the pork is tender. Stir in the vinegar and the pineapple fruit and heat through for 5 minutes. Serve sprinkled with the scallions.

SERVES 4

1 lb/450 g lean boneless pork

1½ tbsp all-purpose flour

1 tsp ground coriander

1 tsp ground cumin

1½ tsp ground cinnamon

1 tbsp olive oil

1 onion, chopped

14 oz/400 g canned chopped tomatoes

2 tbsp tomato paste

1¼–scant 2 cups chicken stock

8 oz/225 g carrots, chopped

12 oz/350 g squash, such as kabocha, peeled, seeded, and chopped

8 oz/225 g leeks, sliced, blanched, and drained

4 oz/115 g okra, trimmed and sliced

salt and pepper

sprigs of fresh parsley, to garnish

couscous, to serve

Pork and Vegetable Stew

The squash used in this recipe is sometimes quite difficult to find. If that's the case, substitute with either acorn or butternut squash.

• Trim off any fat or gristle from the pork and cut into thin strips about 2 inches/5 cm long. Mix the flour and spices together. Toss the pork in the spiced flour until well coated and reserve any remaining spiced flour.

• Heat the oil in a large, heavy-bottom pan and cook the onion, stirring frequently, for 5 minutes, or until softened. Add the pork and cook over high heat, stirring frequently, for 5 minutes, or until browned on all sides and sealed. Sprinkle in the reserved spiced flour and cook, stirring constantly, for 2 minutes, then remove from the heat.

• Gradually add the tomatoes to the pan. Blend the tomato paste with a little of the stock in a pitcher and gradually stir into the pan, then stir in half the remaining stock.

• Add the carrots, then return to the heat and bring to a boil, stirring. Reduce the heat, then cover and simmer, stirring occasionally, for 1½ hours. Add the squash and cook for an additional 15 minutes.

• Add the leeks and okra, and the remaining stock if you prefer a thinner ragoût. Simmer for an additional 15 minutes, or until the pork and vegetables are tender. Season to taste with salt and pepper, then garnish with fresh parsley and serve with couscous.

SERVES 4

1–1 lb 4 oz/450–550 g lean ham
1–2 tbsp olive oil, plus 1–2 tsp
1 onion, chopped
2–3 garlic cloves, chopped
2 celery stalks, chopped
6 oz/175 g sliced carrots
1 cinnamon stick, bruised
½ tsp ground cloves
¼ tsp freshly grated nutmeg
1 tsp dried oregano, plus a sprig of fresh oregano to garnish
scant 2 cups chicken stock or vegetable stock
1–2 tbsp maple syrup
3 large, spicy sausages, about 8 oz/225 g, or chorizo (outer casing removed)
14 oz/400 g canned black-eye peas or fava beans
1 orange bell pepper
1 tbsp cornstarch
pepper
creamed mashed potatoes, to serve

Ham with Black-Eye Peas

In order to get the maximum flavor from a cinnamon stick, it is a good idea to bruise it lightly. Simply crush the cinnamon stick in your hands very gently without breaking it up altogether. This really does help to release the delicate taste.

• Trim off any fat or skin from the ham and cut into 1½-inch/4-cm chunks. Heat 1 tablespoon oil in a heavy-bottom pan and cook the ham over high heat, stirring frequently, for 5 minutes, or until browned on all sides and sealed. Using a slotted spoon, remove from the pan and set aside.

• Add the onion, garlic, celery, and carrots to the pan with an additional 1 tablespoon oil if necessary and cook over medium heat, stirring frequently, for 5 minutes, or until softened. Add all the spices and season with pepper to taste, then cook, stirring constantly, for 2 minutes.

• Return the ham to the pan. Add the dried oregano, stock, and maple syrup to taste, then bring to a boil, stirring. Reduce the heat, then cover and simmer, stirring occasionally, for 1 hour.

• Heat the remaining 1–2 teaspoons oil in a skillet and cook the sausages, turning frequently, until browned all over. Remove and cut each into 3–4 chunks, then add to the pan. Drain and rinse the peas, then drain again.

• Seed and chop the orange bell pepper. Add the beans and bell pepper to the pan, and simmer for an additional 20 minutes. Blend 2 tablespoons of water with the cornstarch and stir into the stew, then cook for 3–5 minutes.

• Discard the cinnamon stick. Serve garnished with the sprig of oregano and accompanied by creamed mashed potatoes and green vegetables.

Poultry, and chicken in particular, is a sure-fire winner, because it always tastes good and is universally popular with even the most cautious of meat-eaters, including children. Its easy-going texture makes it easy to digest, and it is lean and healthy, especially when the skin is removed. When it comes to stews and casseroles, it is also highly versatile, since chicken portions, a whole chicken divided into pieces, or chunks of chicken can be used. Chicken portions with bones obviously take longer to cook than boneless chunks, but the cooking time is still far less than for other meat, so it is ideal for when a shorter cooking time is required. But whenever cooking whole portions of chicken, always ensure that they are thoroughly cooked by inserting a skewer into the thickest part of the meat and checking that the juices run clear. If they are pink, additional cooking is needed.

POULTRY AND GAME

Game offers an extra dimension in stews and casseroles, with its more complex, fulsome taste and robust texture producing a rich, sophisticated result. Here we feature pheasant and duck as well as venison.

Again, flavors are drawn from around the globe in these recipes. Rich and creamy Chicken in White Wine is Alsace's answer to Coq au Vin, while Florida Chicken speaks for itself, its name referring to the fresh orange flesh and juice used to complement the delicate taste of chicken so well. On the game side, duck is the main ingredient of a Creole classic, Duck Jambalaya-Style Stew, along with its traditional additions of ham, tomatoes, green bell pepper, and rice, all spiked with chili.

SERVES 4

4 chicken portions, about 5½ oz/150 g each
1½ tbsp all-purpose flour
2 tbsp olive oil
1 onion, chopped
2–3 garlic cloves, chopped
1 fresh red chili, seeded and chopped
8 oz/225 g chorizo, outer casing removed, or spicy sausages, cut into small chunks
1¼ cups chicken stock
⅔ cup white wine or additional chicken stock
1 tbsp dark soy sauce
1 large red bell pepper, seeded and sliced into rings
2 cups frozen or shelled fresh fava beans, thawed if frozen
1 oz/25 g arugula or baby spinach leaves
salt and pepper
long-grain rice, to serve

Chicken with Red Bell Pepper and Fava Beans

If using frozen fava beans in this dish, thawing them beforehand is a good idea. otherwise, adding frozen beans to the casserole will lower the temperature of the dish and the chicken could take longer to cook.

• Preheat the oven to 375°F/190°C. Lightly rinse the chicken and pat dry with paper towels. Season the flour well with salt and pepper. Toss the chicken in the seasoned flour until well coated and reserve any remaining seasoned flour.

• Heat half the oil in a large, heavy-bottom skillet and cook the chicken over medium-high heat, turning frequently, for 10 minutes, or until golden all over and sealed, adding more of the remaining oil if necessary. Using a slotted spoon, transfer to an ovenproof casserole.

• Add the remaining oil to the skillet and cook the onion, garlic, and chili over medium heat, stirring frequently, for 5 minutes, or until softened. Add the chorizo and cook, stirring frequently, for 2 minutes. Sprinkle in the reserved seasoned flour and cook, stirring constantly, for 2 minutes, then remove from the heat. Gradually stir in the stock, wine, and soy sauce, then return to the heat and bring to a boil, stirring.

• Pour over the chicken in the casserole, then cover and cook in the preheated oven for 25 minutes. Add the red bell pepper and cook for an additional 10 minutes. Add the fava beans and cook for an additional 10 minutes, or until the chicken and vegetables are tender and the chicken juices run clear when a skewer is inserted into the thickest part of the meat.

• Remove from the oven. Taste and adjust the seasoning, then stir in the arugula and let stand for 2 minutes, or until wilted. Serve with rice.

SERVES 4

1 tbsp unsalted butter
2 tbsp olive oil
4 lb/1.8 kg skinned, unboned chicken portions
2 red onions, sliced
2 garlic cloves, finely chopped
14 oz/400 g canned chopped tomatoes
2 tbsp chopped fresh flat-leaf parsley
6 fresh basil leaves, torn
2/3 cup red wine
8 oz/225 g mushrooms, sliced
salt and pepper

Hunter's Chicken

Try substituting Marsala for the red wine, and adding 1 seeded and sliced green bell pepper with the onions.

• Preheat the oven to 325°F/160°C. Heat the butter and oil in a flameproof casserole and cook the chicken over medium-high heat, turning frequently, for 10 minutes, or until golden all over and sealed. Using a slotted spoon, transfer to a plate.

• Add the onions and garlic to the casserole and cook over low heat, stirring occasionally, for 10 minutes, or until softened and golden. Add the tomatoes with their juice, the herbs, sun-dried tomato paste, and wine, and season to taste with salt and pepper. Bring to a boil, then return the chicken portions to the casserole, pushing them down into the sauce.

• Cover and cook in the preheated oven for 50 minutes. Add the mushrooms and cook for an additional 10 minutes, or until the chicken is tender and the juices run clear when a skewer is inserted into the thickest part of the meat. Serve immediately.

SERVES 4

4 chicken portions, about 5½ oz/150 g each
1 tbsp all-purpose flour
2½ tbsp olive oil
8–12 shallots, halved if large
2–4 garlic cloves, sliced
1¾ cups chicken stock
¼ cup sherry
few sprigs fresh thyme, plus 1 tbsp chopped fresh thyme to garnish
4 oz/115 g cherry tomatoes
4 oz/115 g baby corn, halved lengthwise
2 large slices white or whole-wheat bread
salt and pepper

Poulet Marengo-Style

After cooking and while still hot, you can toss the croutons in finely chopped fresh thyme or finely grated Parmesan cheese for additional flavor.

- Lightly rinse the chicken and pat dry with paper towels. Season the flour well with salt and pepper. Toss the chicken in the seasoned flour until well coated and reserve any remaining seasoned flour.
- Heat 1 tablespoon of the oil in a large, deep skillet and cook the chicken over medium-high heat, turning frequently, for 10 minutes, or until golden all over and sealed. Using a slotted spoon, transfer to a plate.
- Add the shallots and garlic to the skillet and cook over medium heat, stirring frequently, for 5 minutes, or until softened. Sprinkle in the reserved seasoned flour and cook, stirring constantly, for 2 minutes, then remove from the heat. Gradually stir in the stock followed by the sherry, then return to the heat and bring to a boil, stirring.
- Return the chicken to the skillet and add the thyme sprigs. Reduce the heat, then cover and simmer, stirring occasionally, for 40 minutes. Add the tomatoes and baby corn and simmer for an additional 10 minutes, or until the chicken is tender and the juices run clear when a skewer is inserted into the thickest part of the meat.
- Meanwhile, cut the bread into small cubes. Heat the remaining oil in a skillet and cook the bread, stirring frequently, for 4–5 minutes, or until golden. Serve the stew garnished with the chopped thyme and the croutons.

SERVES 6

- 4 lb/1.8 kg chicken portions
- 2 tbsp paprika
- 2 tbsp olive oil
- 2 tbsp butter
- 1 lb/450 g onions
- 2 yellow bell peppers
- 14 oz/400 g canned chopped tomatoes
- scant 1 cup dry white wine
- scant 2 cups chicken stock
- 1 tbsp Worcestershire sauce
- ½ tsp Tabasco sauce
- 1 tbsp finely chopped fresh parsley
- 11½ oz/325 g canned corn kernels, drained
- 15 oz/425 g canned lima beans, drained and rinsed
- 2 tbsp all-purpose flour
- 4 tbsp water
- salt
- fresh sprigs of parsley, to garnish

Brunswick Stew

If you decide to substitute fresh tomatoes for canned tomatoes in a stew, add 1 tablespoon of tomato paste to the dish at the same time, to make sure that the flavor is strong enough.

• Season the chicken to taste with salt, and dust with the paprika.

• Heat the oil and butter in a flameproof casserole or large pan and cook the chicken over medium-high heat, turning frequently, for 10 minutes, or until golden all over and sealed. Using a slotted spoon, transfer to a plate.

• Chop the onions and seed and chop the yellow bell peppers, then add them to the casserole and cook over medium heat, stirring frequently, for 5 minutes, or until softened. Add the tomatoes, wine, stock, Worcestershire sauce, Tabasco sauce, and parsley and bring to a boil, stirring. Return the chicken to the casserole, then cover and simmer, stirring occasionally, for 30 minutes.

• Add the corn and lima beans to the casserole, then partially re-cover and simmer for an additional 30 minutes. Put the flour and water in a small bowl and blend to make a paste. Stir a ladleful of the cooking liquid into the paste, then stir it into the stew. Cook, stirring frequently, for 5 minutes, or until thickened. Serve garnished with parsley sprigs.

SERVES 4

4 chicken portions, about 5½ oz/150 g each, skinned if preferred
1 tbsp olive oil
1 onion, chopped
2 celery stalks, coarsely chopped
1½ tbsp all-purpose flour
1¼ cups clear apple juice
⅔ cup chicken stock
1 baking apple, cored and cut into fourths
2 bay leaves
1–2 tsp clear honey
1 yellow bell pepper, seeded and cut into chunks
1 tbsp butter
1 large or 2 medium eating apples, cored and sliced
2 tbsp raw brown sugar
salt and pepper
1 tbsp chopped fresh mint, to garnish

Chicken and Apple Pot

You could add a couple of tablespoons of Calvados—a dry apple brandy from Normandy in France—to intensify the apple flavors in this dish.

• Preheat the oven to 375°F/190°C. Lightly rinse the chicken and pat dry with paper towels.
• Heat the oil in a deep skillet and cook the chicken over medium-high heat, turning frequently, for 10 minutes, or until golden all over and sealed. Using a slotted spoon, transfer to an ovenproof casserole.
• Add the onion and celery to the skillet and cook over medium heat, stirring frequently, for 5 minutes, or until softened. Sprinkle in the flour and cook, stirring constantly, for 2 minutes, then remove from the heat.
• Gradually stir in the apple juice and stock, then return to the heat and bring to a boil, stirring. Add the cooking apple, bay leaves, and honey and season to taste.
• Pour over the chicken in the casserole, then cover and cook in the preheated oven for 25 minutes. Add the bell pepper and cook for an additional 10–15 minutes, or until the chicken is tender and the juices run clear when a skewer is inserted into the thickest part of the meat.
• Meanwhile, preheat the broiler to high. Melt the butter in a pan over low heat. Line the broiler pan with kitchen foil. Brush the eating apple slices with half the butter, then sprinkle with a little sugar and cook under the broiler for 2–3 minutes, or until the sugar has caramelized. Turn the slices over. Brush with the remaining butter and sprinkle with the remaining sugar, and cook for an additional 2 minutes. Serve the stew garnished with the apple slices and mint.

SERVES 4–6

1 chicken, weighing 3 lb 8 oz/1.6 kg, cut into 8 pieces, or 8 chicken thighs
2 tbsp all-purpose flour
4 tbsp unsalted butter
1 tbsp corn oil
4 shallots, finely chopped
12 white mushrooms, sliced
2 tbsp brandy
generous 2 cups Riesling white wine
1 cup heavy cream
salt and pepper
chopped fresh flat-leaf parsley, to garnish

Chicken in White Wine

Take great care when igniting the brandy and use a long-handled match. Set light to the fumes rather than the actual brandy.

• Put the chicken and flour, with salt and pepper to taste, in a plastic bag, then hold the top closed and shake until the chicken pieces are lightly coated all over. Remove the chicken from the bag, shake off any excess flour, and set aside.

• Heat 2 tbsp of the butter and all of the oil in a large sauté pan or skillet with a tight-fitting lid, or a flameproof casserole, and cook the chicken over medium-high heat, turning frequently, for 10 minutes, or until golden all over and sealed. Using a slotted spoon, transfer to a plate.

• Pour off all the fat in the pan and wipe the pan with paper towels. Heat the remaining butter in the pan over medium-high heat. When the butter stops foaming, cook the shallots and mushrooms, stirring constantly, for 3 minutes, or until the shallots are golden and the mushrooms are lightly browned.

• Return the chicken to the pan and remove the pan from the heat. Warm the brandy in a ladle or small pan, then ignite and pour it over the chicken to flambé.

• When the flames die down, return the pan to the heat, then pour in the wine and slowly bring to a boil, scraping any sediment from the bottom of the pan. Reduce the heat to low, then cover and simmer for 40–45 minutes, or until the chicken is tender and the juices run clear when a skewer is inserted into the thickest part of the meat. Meanwhile, preheat the oven to its lowest temperature. Using a slotted spoon, transfer the chicken to a large serving platter and keep it warm in the oven.

• Tilt the pan and use a large metal spoon to remove the fat from the surface of the cooking liquid. Stir in the cream and bring the sauce to a boil. The sauce will boil quickly and should reduce by half almost instantly. Add salt and pepper to taste.

• To serve, spoon the sauce with the mushrooms and shallots over the chicken and garnish with the parsley.

SERVES 4

1 lb/450 g skinless, boneless chicken
1½ tbsp all-purpose flour
1 tbsp olive oil
1 onion, cut into wedges
2 celery stalks, sliced
⅔ cup orange juice
1¼ cups chicken stock
1 tbsp light soy sauce
1–2 tsp clear honey
1 tbsp grated orange rind
1 orange bell pepper, seeded and chopped
8 oz/225 g zucchini, sliced into half moons
2 small corncobs, halved, or 3½ oz/100 g baby corn
1 orange, peeled and segmented
salt and pepper
1 tbsp chopped fresh parsley, to garnish

Florida Chicken

Instead of using honey, try maple syrup to add an extra dimension to the flavor.

• Lightly rinse the chicken and pat dry with paper towels. Cut into bite-size pieces. Season the flour well with salt and pepper. Toss the chicken in the seasoned flour until well coated and reserve any remaining seasoned flour.

• Heat the oil in a large, heavy-bottom skillet and cook the chicken over high heat, stirring frequently, for 5 minutes, or until golden on all sides and sealed. Using a slotted spoon, transfer to a plate.

• Add the onion and celery to the skillet and cook over medium heat, stirring frequently, for 5 minutes, or until softened. Sprinkle in the reserved seasoned flour and cook, stirring constantly, for 2 minutes, then remove from the heat. Gradually stir in the orange juice, stock, soy sauce, and honey followed by the orange rind, then return to the heat and bring to a boil, stirring.

• Return the chicken to the skillet. Reduce the heat, then cover and simmer, stirring occasionally, for 15 minutes. Add the orange pepper, zucchini, and corncob and simmer for an additional 10 minutes, or until the chicken and vegetables are tender. Add the orange segments, then stir well and heat through for 1 minute. Serve garnished with the parsley.

SERVES 4

4 duck portions, about 5½ oz/150 g each
1–2 tsp olive oil, plus 1 tbsp (optional)
1 red onion, cut into wedges
2–3 garlic cloves, chopped
1 large carrot, chopped
2 celery stalks, chopped
2 tbsp all-purpose flour
1¼ cups red wine, such as claret
2 tbsp brandy (optional)
⅔–generous ¾ cup stock or water
3-inch/7.5-cm strip of orange rind
2 tsp redcurrant jelly
4 oz/115 g sugarsnap peas
4 oz/115 g white mushrooms
salt and pepper
1 tbsp chopped fresh parsley, to garnish

Duck and Red Wine Stew

If using duck breasts only, the cooking time can be reduced by about 15 minutes.

• Remove and discard the fat from the duck. Lightly rinse and pat dry with paper towels.

• Heat a large, deep skillet for 1 minute until warm but not piping hot. Put the duck portions in the skillet and heat gently until the fat starts to run. Increase the heat a little, then cook, turning over halfway through, for 5 minutes, or until browned on both sides and sealed. Using a slotted spoon, transfer the duck portions to a flameproof casserole.

• Add 1 tablespoon of the oil if there is little duck fat in the skillet and cook the onion, garlic, carrot, and celery, stirring frequently, for 5 minutes, or until softened. Sprinkle in the flour and cook, stirring constantly, for 2 minutes, then remove the skillet from the heat.

• Gradually stir in the wine, brandy (if using), and stock, then return to the heat and bring to a boil, stirring. Season to taste with salt and pepper, then add the orange rind and redcurrant jelly. Pour over the duck portions in the casserole, then cover and simmer, stirring occasionally, for 1–1¼ hours.

• Cook the sugarsnap peas in a pan of boiling water for 3 minutes, then drain and add to the stew. Meanwhile, heat 1–2 teaspoons of the olive oil in a small pan and cook the mushrooms, stirring frequently, for 3 minutes, or until beginning to soften. Add to the stew. Cook the stew for an additional 5 minutes, or until the duck is tender. Serve garnished with the parsley.

SERVES 4

4 duck breasts, about 5½ oz/150 g each
2 tbsp olive oil
8 oz/225 g piece ham, cut into small chunks
8 oz/225 g chorizo, outer casing removed
1 onion, chopped
3 garlic cloves, chopped
3 celery stalks, chopped
1–2 fresh red chilies, seeded and chopped
1 green bell pepper, seeded and chopped
2½ cups chicken stock
1 tbsp chopped fresh oregano
14 oz/400 g canned chopped tomatoes
1–2 tsp hot pepper sauce, or to taste
salt
fresh sprigs of parsley, to garnish

TO SERVE

green salad
long-grain rice

Duck Jambalaya-Style Stew

This is a great dish to serve at an informal supper party, with plenty of salad and crusty bread. Use a large deep dish for serving it and put the rice in first, then spoon over the Jambalaya. Serve with chilled beer or white wine.

• Remove and discard the skin and any fat from the duck breasts. Cut the flesh into bite-size pieces.
• Heat half the oil in a large deep skillet and cook the duck, ham, and chorizo over high heat, stirring frequently, for 5 minutes, or until browned on all sides and sealed. Using a slotted spoon, remove from the skillet and set aside.
• Add the onion, garlic, celery, and chili to the skillet and cook over medium heat, stirring frequently, for 5 minutes, or until softened. Add the green bell pepper, then stir in the stock, oregano, tomatoes, and hot pepper sauce.
• Bring to a boil, then reduce the heat and return the duck, ham, and chorizo to the skillet. Cover and simmer, stirring occasionally, for 20 minutes, or until the duck and ham are tender.
• Drain and serve with the Jambalaya, garnished with parsley and accompanied by a green salad and rice.

SERVES 6

3 tbsp olive oil

2 lb 4 oz/1 kg casserole venison, cut into 1¼-inch/3-cm cubes

2 onions, finely sliced

2 garlic cloves, chopped

1½ cups beef stock or vegetable stock

2 tbsp all-purpose flour

½ cup port or red wine

2 tbsp redcurrant jelly

6 juniper berries, crushed

4 cloves, crushed

pinch of cinnamon

small grating of nutmeg

salt and pepper

baked or mashed potatoes, to serve

Venison Casserole

This casserole benefits from being made the day before to let the flavors develop. Ensure that you cool the casserole as quickly as possible and store, covered, in the refrigerator or a cool larder overnight. Reheat gently before serving, on the stove or in the oven at 350°F/180°C for 35–40 minutes.

- Preheat the oven to 350°F/180°C. Heat the oil in a large skillet and cook the venison over high heat, stirring frequently, for 5 minutes, or until browned on all sides and sealed. Using a slotted spoon, transfer to a casserole.
- Add the onions and garlic to the skillet and cook over medium heat, stirring frequently, for 5 minutes, or until softened, then transfer to the casserole.
- Gradually stir in the stock and scrape any sediment from the bottom of the skillet, then bring to a boil, stirring.
- Sprinkle the flour over the meat in the casserole dish and toss well to coat evenly. Add the hot stock to the casserole and stir well, ensuring that the meat is just covered. Stir in the wine, redcurrant jelly, and spices.
- Season well with salt and pepper, then cover and cook in the center of the preheated oven for 2–2½ hours.
- Check and adjust the seasoning if necessary, then serve piping hot with baked or mashed potatoes.

SERVES 4

½ oz/15 g dried cèpes or porcini mushrooms
1 hen pheasant, weighing about 2 lb 12 oz/1.25 kg
2 tbsp all-purpose flour
2 tbsp olive oil
1 onion, chopped
1 large carrot, thinly sliced
2 celery stalks, sliced
scant 2 cups chicken stock
1 fresh bouquet garni
1–2 tsp redcurrant jelly
2–3 tbsp port
1 tbsp butter or margarine
2 cups sliced mushrooms
½ cup no-soak prunes, chopped
salt and pepper
1 tbsp chopped fresh parsley, to garnish

TO SERVE

creamed potato and parsnip mash
red cabbage
peas

Pheasant with Mushrooms

Ask your butcher or supplier to joint the pheasant for you. This recipe will also work well with other sorts of game, such as venison or duck.

• Preheat the oven to 350°F/180°C. Put the dried mushrooms in a heatproof pitcher, then cover with almost boiling water and let stand for 20 minutes to soak. Discard any excess fat from the pheasant, then lightly rinse and pat dry with paper towels, and cut into 4 pieces. Season the flour well with salt and pepper. Toss the pheasant in the seasoned flour until well coated and reserve any remaining seasoned flour.

• Heat all but 2 teaspoons of the oil in a large skillet and cook the pheasant over medium-high heat, turning frequently, for 10 minutes, or until browned all over and sealed. Using a slotted spoon, transfer the pheasant to an ovenproof casserole.

• Add the remaining oil to the skillet and cook the onion, carrot, and celery over medium heat, stirring frequently, for 5 minutes, or until softened. Sprinkle in the reserved seasoned flour and cook, stirring constantly, for 2 minutes, then remove from the heat. Gradually stir in the stock followed by the soaked dried mushrooms and their soaking liquid, then return to the heat and bring to a boil, stirring.

• Pour over the pheasant in the casserole and add the bouquet garni, redcurrant jelly, and port. Cover and cook in the preheated oven for 1½ hours.

• Melt the butter in a pan and cook the mushrooms, stirring frequently, for 3 minutes, or until beginning to soften. Add to the casserole with the prunes and cook for an additional 15–20 minutes, or until the pheasant is tender. Serve garnished with parsley, accompanied by potato and parsnip mash, red cabbage, and peas.

It may seem surprising to some people to feature fish and shellfish in a book of stews and casseroles, but in fact there are many traditional stew recipes from around the Mediterranean that consist largely of fish, with vegetables playing a supporting role. This is not so surprising, really, when you consider the abundance of seafood and array of colorful, sun-ripened vegetables that the region has to offer. In addition to the classic Mediterranean dishes, this chapter includes several recipes from the East, with their characteristically aromatic flavors, along with a piquant taste of Creole cooking from Louisiana. If you cannot find a particular fish, it is worth finding alternatives. For seafood stews, many fish are suitable, including shellfish. It is worth keeping in mind that fish should not flake too much by overcooking and that oily fish may not always be suitable.

SIMMERING SEAFOOD

When cooking fish and shellfish stews and casseroles, it is best to prepare all the ingredients before starting to cook the dish, since these star items take a short time and their flavor and texture will be easily impaired if overcooked. Also these dishes should be eaten as soon as they have been cooked, and not reheated. If using frozen fish, it is worth thawing the fish slowly, letting it stand on a plate, lightly covered, in the refrigerator overnight. The next day, rinse lightly, then pat dry with paper towels and return to the refrigerator until required.

Many of these dishes contain shrimp. To shell and devein them, remove the head and tail, then peel away the shell. Using a sharp knife, cut along the back of the shrimp to remove the black intestinal thread that runs down the center, then rinse well.

Entertain your friends in style with these exotic meals, or give your family a treat and keep them coming back for more!

Bouillabaisse

SERVES 8

2 lb 12 oz/1.25 kg sea bass, filleted, skinned, and cut into bite-size chunks

2 lb 12 oz/1.25 kg redfish, filleted, skinned, and cut into bite-size chunks

3 tbsp extra-virgin olive oil

grated rind of 1 orange

1 garlic clove, finely chopped

pinch of saffron threads

2 tbsp pastis, such as Pernod

1 lb/450 g live mussels

1 large cooked crab

1 small fennel bulb, finely chopped

2 celery stalks, finely chopped

1 onion, finely chopped

5 cups fish stock

8 oz/225 g small new potatoes, scrubbed

8 oz/225 g tomatoes, peeled, seeded, and chopped

1 lb/450 g large raw shrimp, shelled and deveined

salt and pepper

Redfish, or Norwegian haddock, is related to the scorpion fish. It is a traditional ingredient in bouillabaisse, but if you cannot find it, use red snapper instead.

• Put the fish pieces in a large bowl and add 2 tablespoons of the oil, and the orange rind, garlic, saffron, and pastis. Toss the fish pieces until well coated, then cover and let marinate in the refrigerator for 30 minutes.

• Meanwhile, clean the mussels by scrubbing or scraping the shells and pulling out any beards that are attached to them. Discard any with broken shells or any that refuse to close when tapped. Remove the meat from the crab, then chop and reserve.

• Heat the remaining oil in a large, flameproof casserole and cook the fennel, celery, and onion over low heat, stirring occasionally, for 5 minutes, or until softened. Add the stock and bring to a boil. Add the potatoes and tomatoes and cook over medium heat for 7 minutes.

• Reduce the heat and add the fish to the stew, beginning with the thickest pieces, then add the mussels, shrimp, and crab and simmer until the fish is opaque, the mussels have opened, and the shrimp have turned pink. Discard any mussels that remain closed. Season to taste with salt and pepper and serve immediately.

SERVES 4

1 yellow bell pepper, 1 red bell pepper, 1 orange bell pepper, seeded and cut into fourths
1 lb/450 g ripe tomatoes
2 large, fresh, mild green chilies, such as poblano
6 garlic cloves, peeled but kept whole
2 tsp dried oregano or dried mixed herbs
2 tbsp olive oil, plus extra for drizzling
1 large onion, finely chopped
scant 2 cups fish stock, vegetable or chicken stock
finely grated rind and juice of 1 lime
2 tbsp chopped fresh cilantro, plus extra to garnish
1 bay leaf
1 lb/450 g red snapper fillets, skinned and cut into chunks
8 oz/225 g raw shrimp, shelled and deveined
8 oz/225 g raw squid rings
salt and pepper
warmed flour tortillas, to serve

South-Western Seafood Stew

Roasting the bell peppers, tomatoes, chilies, and garlic enhances the flavor of this sumptuous seafood medley. You can use any other firm fish fillets or a mixture, if you prefer.

• Preheat the oven to 400°F/200°C. Put the pepper fourths, skin-side up, in a roasting pan with the tomatoes, chilies, and garlic. Sprinkle with the oregano and drizzle with oil. Roast in the preheated oven for 30 minutes, or until the bell peppers are well browned and softened.

• Remove the roasted vegetables from the oven and let stand until cool enough to handle. Peel off the skins from the bell peppers, tomatoes, and chilies and chop the flesh. Finely chop the garlic.

• Heat the oil in a large pan and cook the onion, stirring frequently, for 5 minutes, or until softened. Add the bell peppers, tomatoes, chilies, garlic, stock, lime rind and juice, cilantro, bay leaf, and salt and pepper to taste. Bring to a boil, then stir in the seafood. Reduce the heat, then cover and simmer gently for 10 minutes, or until the fish and squid is just cooked through and the shrimp have turned pink. Discard the bay leaf, then garnish with chopped cilantro before serving, accompanied by warmed flour tortillas.

SERVES 4–6

large pinch of saffron threads

4 tbsp almost boiling water

6 tbsp olive oil

1 large onion, chopped

2 garlic cloves, finely chopped

1½ tbsp chopped fresh thyme leaves

2 bay leaves

2 red bell peppers, seeded and coarsely chopped

1 lb 12 oz/800 g canned chopped tomatoes

1 tsp smoked paprika

1 cup fish stock

1 cup blanched almonds, toasted and finely ground

12–16 live mussels

12–16 live clams

1 lb 5 oz/600 g thick boned hake or cod fillets, skinned and cut into 2-inch/5-cm chunks

12–16 raw shrimp, shelled and deveined

salt and pepper

thick crusty bread, to serve

Spanish Fish Stew

Take care not to overcook the hake, or it will break into flakes that have very little texture. Angler fish is an excellent alternative to hake or cod.

• Put the saffron threads in a heatproof pitcher with the water and let stand for at least 10 minutes to infuse.

• Heat the oil in a large, heavy-bottom flameproof casserole over medium-high heat. Reduce the heat to low and cook the onion, stirring occasionally, for 10 minutes, or until golden but not browned. Stir in the garlic, thyme, bay leaves, and red bell peppers and cook, stirring frequently, for 5 minutes, or until the bell peppers are softened and the onions have softened further.

• Add the tomatoes and paprika and simmer, stirring frequently, for an additional 5 minutes.

• Stir in the stock, the saffron and its soaking liquid, and the almonds and bring to a boil, stirring. Reduce the heat and simmer for 5–10 minutes, or until the sauce reduces and thickens. Season to taste with salt and pepper.

• Meanwhile, clean the mussels and clams by scrubbing or scraping the shells and pulling out any beards that are attached to the mussels. Discard any with broken shells or any that refuse to close when tapped.

• Gently stir the hake into the stew so that it doesn't break up, then add the shrimp, mussels, and clams. Reduce the heat to very low, then cover and simmer for 5 minutes, or until the hake is opaque, the mussels and clams have opened, and the shrimp have turned pink. Discard any mussels or clams that remain closed. Serve immediately with plenty of thick crusty bread for soaking up the juices.

SERVES 4–6

large pinch of saffron threads

2 lb/900 g fresh Mediterranean fish, such as sea bass, angler fish, red snapper or haddock

24 large raw shrimp in their shells

1 raw squid

2 tbsp olive oil

1 large onion, finely chopped

1 fennel bulb, thinly sliced, feathery fronds reserved

2 large garlic cloves, crushed

4 tbsp pastis, such as Pernod

4 cups fish stock

2 large sun-ripened tomatoes, peeled, seeded, and diced, or 14 oz/400 g chopped tomatoes, drained

1 tbsp tomato paste

1 bay leaf

pinch of sugar

pinch of dried chili flakes (optional)

salt and pepper

French bread, to serve

Marseille-Style Fish Stew

Use whatever fish is available, but avoid using oily fish such as mackerel and salmon, or swordfish and tuna, which are too meaty for this treatment. Scallops and mussels are suitable shellfish to use in this dish.

- Put the saffron threads in a small dry skillet over high heat and toast, stirring constantly, for 1 minute, or until you can smell the aroma. Immediately tip out of the skillet and set aside.
- Prepare the fish as necessary, removing and reserving all skin, bones, and heads. Cut the flesh into large chunks. Shell and devein the shrimp. Cover and refrigerate the fish and shrimp until required.
- To prepare the squid, use your fingers to rub off the thin membrane that covers the body. Pull the head and insides out of the body sac, then cut off and reserve the tentacles. Pull out the thin, clear quill that is inside the body. Rinse the squid inside and out, then cut the body into 1/4-inch/5-mm rings. Cover and refrigerate the squid until required.
- Heat the oil in a large, flameproof casserole or heavy-bottom pan and cook the onion and sliced fennel for 3 minutes. Add the garlic and cook for an additional 5 minutes, or until the onion and fennel are softened but not browned.
- Remove the casserole from the heat. Warm the pastis in a ladle or small pan, then ignite and pour over the onion and fennel to flambé.
- When the flames die down, return the casserole to the heat and stir in the stock, tomatoes, tomato paste, bay leaf, sugar, chili flakes, if using, and salt and pepper to taste. Slowly bring to a boil, then reduce the heat and simmer for 15 minutes. Taste and adjust the seasoning if necessary.
- Add the shrimp and squid and simmer just until the shrimp have turned pink and the squid is opaque. Using a slotted spoon, transfer the shrimp and squid to warmed serving bowls.
- Add the fish to the broth and simmer just until the flesh flakes easily—not longer than 5 minutes, depending on the type of fish. Transfer the seafood and broth to the serving bowls, removing the smaller, thinner pieces first. Garnish with the reserved fennel fronds and serve with French bread.

SERVES 6

2 tbsp sunflower-seed or corn oil
6 oz/175 g okra, trimmed and cut into 1-inch/2.5-cm pieces
2 onions, finely chopped
4 celery stalks, very finely chopped
1 garlic clove, finely chopped
2 tbsp all-purpose flour
½ tsp sugar
1 tsp ground cumin
3 cups fish stock
1 red bell pepper and 1 green bell pepper, seeded and chopped
2 large tomatoes, chopped
12 oz/350 g large raw shrimp
4 tbsp chopped fresh parsley
1 tbsp chopped fresh cilantro
dash of Tabasco sauce
12 oz/350 g cod or haddock fillets, skinned
12 oz/350 g angler fish fillet
salt and pepper

Louisiana Gumbo

To shell and devein shrimp, remove the head and tail, then peel away the shell. Using a sharp knife, cut along the back of the prawn to remove the black intestinal thread that runs down the center. Wash well.

• Heat half the oil in a large, flameproof casserole, or large pan with tightly fitting lid, and cook the okra over low heat, stirring frequently, for 5 minutes, or until browned. Using a slotted spoon, remove the okra from the casserole and set aside.

• Heat the remaining oil in the casserole and cook the onion and celery over medium heat, stirring frequently, for 5 minutes, or until softened. Add the garlic and cook, stirring, for 1 minute. Sprinkle in the flour, sugar, and cumin and add salt and pepper to taste. Cook, stirring constantly, for 2 minutes, then remove from the heat.

• Gradually stir in the stock and bring to a boil, stirring. Return the okra to the casserole and add the bell peppers and tomatoes. Partially cover, then reduce the heat to very low and simmer gently, stirring occasionally, for 10 minutes. Meanwhile, shell and devein the shrimp (see left) and reserve.

• Add the herbs and Tabasco sauce to taste. Cut the cod and angler fish into 1-inch/2.5-cm chunks, then gently stir into the stew. Stir in the shrimp. Cover and simmer gently for 5 minutes, or until the fish is cooked through and the shrimp have turned pink. Transfer to a large, warmed serving dish and serve.

SERVES 8

24 live mussels
24 live clams
1 lb/450 g sea bream fillets
6¼ cups fish stock
scant 1 cup dry white wine
2 shallots, finely chopped
24 raw Mediterranean shrimp, shelled and deveined
1 lb 9 oz/700 g tomatoes, peeled, seeded, and coarsely chopped
3 tbsp snipped fresh chives
grated rind of 1 lemon
pinch of saffron threads
3 tbsp finely chopped fresh parsley
salt and pepper

Shellfish Stew

This dish is quite messy, so provide finger bowls filled with hot water and a slice of lemon so that your guests can wash their fingers after eating.

• Clean the mussels and clams by scrubbing or scraping the shells and pulling out any beards that are attached to the mussels. Discard any with broken shells or any that refuse to close when tapped. Cut the sea bream into bite-size pieces.

• Pour the stock and wine into a large, heavy-bottom pan and bring to a boil. Add the mussels, clams, and shallots, then cover and cook over medium heat for 4 minutes. Tip into a strainer, reserving the stock. Discard any mussels or clams that remain closed and set the remainder aside.

• Rinse the pan and strain the stock back into it through a cheesecloth-lined strainer. Return to a boil and add the shrimp and sea bream. Stir in the tomatoes, chives, lemon rind, saffron, and parsley and season to taste with salt and pepper. Simmer gently for 10 minutes, or until the fish flakes easily when tested with the point of a knife.

• Remove the pan from the heat and add the mussels and clams. Cover and let stand for 5 minutes. Divide the stew between 4 soup bowls and serve immediately.

SERVES 4–6

7 oz/200 g dried ribbon egg pasta, such as tagliatelle
2 tbsp butter
1 cup fine fresh bread crumbs
14 fl oz/400 ml canned condensed cream of mushroom soup
½ cup milk
2 celery stalks, chopped
1 red bell pepper, seeded and chopped
1 green bell pepper, seeded and chopped
1¼ cups coarsely grated sharp Cheddar cheese
2 tbsp chopped fresh parsley
7 oz/200 g canned tuna in oil, drained and flaked
salt and pepper

Tuna and Noodle Casserole

If you like the flavor of celery, use canned condensed cream of celery soup instead of the mushroom soup and replace the celery stalks with 7 oz/200 g canned, drained corn kernels.

- Preheat the oven to 400°F/200°C. Bring a large pan of salted water to a boil. Add the pasta, then return to a boil and cook for 2 minutes less than specified on the package directions.
- Meanwhile, melt the butter in a separate pan. Stir in the bread crumbs, then remove from the heat and set aside.
- Drain the pasta well and set aside. Pour the soup into the pasta pan over medium heat, then stir in the milk, celery, bell peppers, half the cheese, and all the parsley. Add the tuna and gently stir in so that the flakes don't break up. Season to taste with salt and pepper. Heat just until small bubbles appear around the edge of the mixture—do not boil.
- Stir the pasta into the pan and use 2 forks to mix all the ingredients together. Spoon the mixture into an ovenproof dish that is also suitable for serving and spread it out.
- Stir the remaining cheese into the buttered bread crumbs, then sprinkle over the top of the pasta mixture. Bake in the preheated oven for 20–25 minutes, or until the topping is golden. Remove from the oven, then let stand for 5 minutes before serving straight from the dish.

Seafood in Saffron Sauce

SERVES 4

8 oz/225 g live clams
8 oz/225 g live mussels
2 tbsp olive oil
1 onion, sliced
pinch of saffron threads
1 tbsp chopped fresh thyme
2 garlic cloves, finely chopped
1 lb 12 oz/800 g canned tomatoes, drained and chopped
¾ cup dry white wine
8 cups fish stock
12 oz/350 g red snapper fillets, cut into bite-size chunks
1 lb/450 g angler fish fillet, cut into bite-size chunks
8 oz/225 g raw squid rings
2 tbsp fresh shredded basil leaves
salt and pepper
fresh bread, to serve

Although saffron is very expensive, its unique aromatic flavor marries particularly well with seafood, and, in any case, you need only a tiny amount.

• Clean the mussels and clams by scrubbing or scraping the shells and pulling out any beards that are attached to the mussels. Discard any with broken shells or any that refuse to close when tapped.
• Heat the oil in a large, flameproof casserole and cook the onion with the saffron, thyme, and a pinch of salt over low heat, stirring occasionally, for 5 minutes, or until softened. Add the garlic and cook, stirring, for 2 minutes.
• Add the tomatoes, wine, and stock, then season to taste with salt and pepper and stir well. Bring to a boil, then reduce the heat and simmer for 15 minutes.
• Add the fish chunks and simmer for an additional 3 minutes. Add the clams, mussels, and squid rings and simmer for an additional 5 minutes, or until the mussels and clams have opened. Discard any that remain closed. Stir in the basil and serve immediately, accompanied by plenty of fresh bread to mop up the broth.

All manner of vegetables can be used and combined to great effect in stews and casseroles, resulting in dishes that are brimming with both flavor and texture. Beans—dried beans, peas, and lentils—are at the heart of many of the recipes in this chapter, and the different types can be interchanged or mixed and matched according to individual preference or availability. If cooking from dried, beans and chickpeas need to be soaked in plenty of cold water for several hours or overnight. Most beans then need to be drained, covered with fresh water, and boiled rapidly for 10 minutes to rid them of potentially harmful substances, before slow cooking—the exact cooking time varying according to the type and age of the beans. However, many different types of beans are conveniently available canned and ready to use, and these are also featured in some of the recipes here.

VITAL VEGETABLES

Lentils, which don't require any presoaking or cooking, take the place of meat in the Vegetable Goulash featured here, accompanied by hearty root vegetables and tender squash in a rich tomato broth. Dried cannellini beans are used in the Spring Stew, but after the initial preparation, this dish is quickly put together, making the best of sweet and tender young vegetables. Canned chickpeas are complemented by eggplant, sweet potatoes, and prunes in the aromatic Moroccan Hot Pot, while tofu is teamed with peppers, green beans, and baby corn in the typically Thai-flavored Fragrant Vegetable Pot.

Whether for everyday eating or informal entertaining, these nutritious and delicious dishes will appeal as much to meat-eaters as vegetarians.

SERVES 4

1⅛ cups fragrant rice
3 tbsp corn oil
9 oz/250 g organic firm tofu
1-inch/2.5-cm piece fresh gingerroot
2 stalks lemongrass
1–2 garlic cloves
1–2 Thai chilies
1 tsp light muscovado sugar
3 shallots, cut into wedges
3 celery stalks
6 oz/175 g carrots
1 red bell pepper,
1 yellow bell pepper
2½–3 cups vegetable stock
2 tbsp light soy sauce
4 oz/115 g green beans
3 oz/85 g broccoli, divided into tiny florets
4 oz/115 g baby corn
6 scallions
1 tbsp fresh cilantro, chopped
1½ tbsp cornstarch
2 tbsp cold water
salt and pepper
long-grain rice, to serve

Fragrant Vegetable Pot

For an even greater variety of vegetables in this dish, add some shredded bok choy and bean sprouts with the scallions and cilantro.

• Bring a large pan of lightly salted water to a boil. Add the rice, then return to a boil and cook for 12 minutes, or until tender but still firm to the bite. Drain, then cover and keep warm.

• Heat 2 tablespoons of the oil in a skillet. Cut the tofu into bite-size cubes, then add to the skillet and cook over low heat, stirring frequently, for 8–10 minutes, or until golden on all sides. Remove and set aside.

• Peel and grate the ginger. Remove the outer leaves of the lemongrass and discard. Finely chop the stalks, crush the garlic, and seed and chop the chilies. Heat the remaining oil in a large, heavy-bottom pan and cook the ginger, lemongrass, garlic, and chilies, stirring frequently, for 3 minutes. Cut the celery into ¼-inch/5-mm slices, and add to the pan with shallots. Cook stirring, for 2 minutes.

• Cut the carrots into batons, then seed the bell peppers and cut them into small chunks. Add the carrots, bell peppers, scant 2 cups of the stock, and soy sauce to the pan, then bring to a boil. Reduce the heat, then cover and simmer for 10 minutes.

• Halve the green beans, and add them to the pan with the broccoli, corn, and the remaining stock and simmer for an additional 5 minutes. Add the tofu, scallions, and cilantro and season to taste with pepper.

• Blend the cornstarch with the water, then stir into the pan and cook, stirring gently to avoid breaking up the vegetables, for 2 minutes, or until the liquid is thickened. Serve immediately with long-grain rice.

SERVES 4

15 oz/425 g canned chickpeas
4 tomatoes, peeled and seeded
3 cups vegetable stock
1 onion, sliced
2 carrots, diagonally sliced
1 tbsp chopped fresh cilantro
6 oz/175 g zucchini, sliced
1 small turnip, cubed
½ tsp ground turmeric
¼ tsp ground ginger
¼ tsp ground cinnamon
8 oz/225 g couscous
salt
fresh sprigs of cilantro, to garnish

Moroccan Vegetable Stew

To peel tomatoes, cut a cross through the skin at the base of each tomato, then put in a heatproof bowl and pour over boiling water. Let stand for a couple of minutes, then drain and plunge into cold water. The skins will peel off easily.

• Drain the chickpeas and rinse under cold running water, then drain again and set aside.
• Coarsely chop the tomatoes and reserve half. Put the remainder in a blender or food processor and process until smooth. Transfer to a large pan and add 1¾ cups of the stock. Bring to a boil, then reduce the heat and add the onion, carrots, chopped cilantro, and salt to taste. Simmer, stirring occasionally, for 10 minutes.
• Stir in the zucchini, turnip, spices, and the reserved tomatoes. Partially cover and simmer for an additional 30 minutes. Stir in the chickpeas and simmer for an additional 5 minutes.
• Meanwhile, bring the remaining stock to a boil in a large, heavy-bottom pan with a tight-fitting lid. Add a pinch of salt, then sprinkle in the couscous, stirring constantly.
• Remove the pan from the heat, then cover and let stand for 5 minutes. Fluff the couscous up with a fork and transfer to 4 serving plates.
• Top with the vegetables and their stock, then garnish with cilantro sprigs and serve immediately.

SERVES 4

1 large fennel bulb
2 tbsp olive oil
1 red onion, cut into small wedges
2–4 garlic cloves, sliced
1 fresh green chili, seeded and chopped
1 small eggplant, about 8 oz/225 g, cut into chunks
2 tbsp tomato paste
scant 2–2½ cups vegetable stock
1 lb/450 g ripe tomatoes
1 tbsp balsamic vinegar
few fresh sprigs of oregano
14 oz/400 g canned cranberry beans
14 oz/400 g canned flageolets
1 yellow bell pepper, seeded and cut into small strips
1 zucchini, sliced into half moons
⅓ cup pitted black olives
25 g/1 oz Parmesan cheese, freshly shaved
salt and pepper
polenta wedges or crusty bread, to serve

Tuscan Bean Stew

Fennel, also known as Florence fennel, has an anise flavor that is excellent when combined with tomatoes, garlic, and chili. If not available, try using some crushed fennel seeds and cook them with the onion and garlic.

• Trim the fennel and reserve any feathery fronds, then cut the bulb into small strips. Heat the oil in a large, heavy-bottom pan with a tight-fitting lid, and cook the onion, garlic, chili, and fennel strips, stirring frequently, for 5–8 minutes, or until softened.

• Add the eggplant and cook, stirring frequently, for 5 minutes. Blend the tomato paste with a little of the stock in a pitcher and pour over the fennel mixture, then add the remaining stock, and the tomatoes, vinegar, and oregano. Bring to a boil, then reduce the heat and simmer, covered, for 15 minutes, or until the tomatoes have begun to collapse.

• Drain and rinse the beans, then drain again. Add them to the pan with the yellow bell pepper, zucchini, and olives. Simmer for an additional 15 minutes, or until the vegetables are tender. Taste and adjust the seasoning. Scatter with the Parmesan shavings and serve garnished with the reserved fennel fronds, accompanied by polenta wedges or crusty bread.

SERVES 4

4 garlic cloves
1 small acorn squash
1 red onion, sliced
2 leeks, sliced
1 eggplant, sliced
1 small celery root, diced
2 turnips, sliced
2 plum tomatoes, chopped
1 carrot, sliced
1 zucchini, sliced
2 red bell peppers
1 fennel bulb, sliced
6 oz/175 g Swiss chard
2 bay leaves
½ tsp fennel seeds
½ tsp chili powder
pinch each of dried thyme, dried oregano, and sugar
½ cup extra-virgin olive oil
scant 1 cup vegetable stock
1 oz/25 g fresh basil leaves, torn
4 tbsp chopped fresh parsley
salt and pepper
2 tbsp freshly grated Parmesan cheese, to serve

Italian Vegetable Stew

Unless you are using beans, nuts, or grains, it is a good idea to complement vegetable dishes with a little cheese to provide some protein.

• Finely chop the garlic and dice the squash. Put them in a large, heavy-bottom pan with a tight-fitting lid. Add the onion, leeks, eggplant, celery root, turnips, tomatoes, carrot, zucchini, red bell peppers, fennel, Swiss chard, bay leaves, fennel seeds, chili powder, thyme, oregano, sugar, oil, stock, and half the basil to the pan. Mix together well, then bring to a boil.

• Reduce the heat, then cover and simmer for 30 minutes, or until all the vegetables are tender.

• Sprinkle in the remaining basil and the parsley and season to taste with salt and pepper. Serve immediately, sprinkled with the cheese.

Chili Bean Stew

SERVES 4–6

- 4 oz/115 g dried kidney beans
- 4 oz/115 g dried chickpeas
- 4 oz/115 g dried cannellini beans
- 2 tbsp olive oil
- 1 onion, chopped
- 2–4 garlic cloves, chopped
- 2 fresh red chilies, seeded and sliced
- 1 tbsp tomato paste
- 3–3¾ cups vegetable stock
- 1 red bell pepper, seeded and chopped
- 4 tomatoes, coarsely chopped
- 1½ cups frozen or shelled fresh fava beans, thawed if frozen
- 1 tbsp chopped fresh cilantro
- pepper
- sour cream, to serve

TO GARNISH

- fresh sprigs of cilantro
- pinch of paprika

If time is short, take a shortcut and instead of the dried beans use double the quantity of canned beans. Disregard the first paragraph and begin at paragraph 2, adding the canned, drained beans in place of the drained, soaked beans. Once the stock is reduced to a simmer, skip the 50 minutes' simmering and move straight to paragraph 3.

• Pick over the beans and rinse thoroughly, then drain and put in separate bowls. Cover with plenty of cold water and let soak overnight. The next day, drain, then put in separate pans and cover with cold water. Bring to a boil and boil rapidly for 10 minutes, then drain and set aside.

• Heat the oil in a large, heavy-bottom pan with a tight-fitting lid, and cook the onion, garlic, and chilies, stirring frequently, for 5 minutes, or until softened. Add the drained soaked beans. Blend the tomato paste with a little of the stock in a pitcher and pour over the bean mixture, then add the remaining stock. Bring to a boil, then reduce the heat and simmer, covered, stirring occasionally, for 50 minutes, or until the beans are almost tender.

• Add the red bell pepper, tomatoes, fava beans, and pepper to taste and simmer for an additional 15–20 minutes, or until the beans are thoroughly cooked. Stir in the chopped cilantro. Serve the stew topped with spoonfuls of sour cream and garnished with sprigs of cilantro and a pinch of paprika.

SERVES 4

12 oz/350 g dried pinto beans, covered with cold water and soaked overnight
2 tbsp olive oil
2 onions, sliced
2 garlic cloves, finely chopped
1 red bell pepper, seeded and sliced
1 yellow bell pepper, seeded and sliced
14 oz/400 g canned chopped tomatoes
2 tbsp tomato paste
1 tbsp torn fresh basil leaves
2 tsp chopped fresh thyme
2 tsp chopped fresh rosemary
1 bay leaf
1/3 cup black olives, pitted and halved
salt and pepper
2 tbsp chopped fresh parsley, to garnish

Provençal Bean Stew

Always follow the package directions for soaking and cooking the particular type of bean you are using. If you use cranberry beans instead of the pinto beans, you will need to boil them vigorously for 10 minutes before simmering.

• Drain the beans and put in a large, heavy-bottom pan, with a tight-fitting lid, then add enough cold water to cover and bring to a boil. Reduce the heat, then cover and simmer for 1 1/4–1 1/2 hours, or until almost tender. Drain, reserving 1 1/4 cups of the cooking liquid.

• Heat the oil in another large, heavy-bottom pan with a tight-fitting lid, and cook the onions, stirring frequently, for 5 minutes, or until softened. Add the garlic and bell peppers and cook, stirring frequently, for 10 minutes.

• Add the tomatoes and their juice, the reserved cooking liquid, tomato paste, herbs, and beans and season to taste with salt and pepper. Cover and simmer for 40 minutes. Add the olives and simmer for an additional 5 minutes. Transfer to a warmed serving dish, then sprinkle with the parsley and serve immediately.

SERVES 4

8 oz/225 g dried cannellini beans
2 tbsp olive oil
4–8 baby onions, halved
2 celery stalks, cut into ¼-inch/5-mm slices
8 oz/225 g baby carrots, scrubbed and halved if large
10½ oz/300 g new potatoes, scrubbed and halved, or cut into fourths if large
3¾–5 cups vegetable stock
1 fresh bouquet garni
1½–2 tbsp light soy sauce
3 oz/85 g baby corn
1 cup frozen or shelled fresh fava beans, thawed if frozen
½–1 savoy or spring (Primo) cabbage, about 8 oz/225 g
1½ tbsp cornstarch
2 tbsp cold water
salt and pepper
2–3 oz/55–85 g Parmesan or sharp Cheddar cheese, grated, to serve

Spring Stew

Although not as widely available as some other varieties of cabbage, savoy cabbage has a delicate flavor that makes it ideal for cooking.

• Pick over the cannellini beans and rinse thoroughly, then drain and put in a large bowl. Cover with plenty of cold water and let soak overnight. The next day, drain, put in a pan and cover with cold water. Bring to a boil and boil rapidly for 10 minutes, then drain and set aside.

• Heat the oil in a large, heavy-bottom pan with a tight-fitting lid, and cook the vegetables, stirring frequently, for 5 minutes, or until softened. Add the stock, drained beans, bouquet garni, and soy sauce, then bring to a boil. Reduce the heat, then cover and simmer for 12 minutes.

• Add the baby corn and fava beans and season to taste with salt and pepper. Simmer for an additional 3 minutes.

• Meanwhile, discard the outer leaves and hard central core from the cabbage and shred the leaves. Add to the pan and simmer for an additional 3–5 minutes, or until all the vegetables are tender.

• Blend the cornstarch with the water, then stir into the pan and cook, stirring, for 4–6 minutes, or until the liquid has thickened. Serve the cheese separately, for stirring into the stew.

SERVES 4

10 cloves
1 onion, peeled but kept whole
1⅛ cups Puy or green lentils
1 bay leaf
6¼ cups vegetable stock
2 leeks, sliced
2 potatoes, diced
2 carrots, chopped
3 zucchini, sliced
1 celery stalk, chopped
1 red bell pepper, seeded and chopped
1 tbsp lemon juice
salt and pepper

Vegetable and Lentil Casserole

Ordinary green lentils are fine to use in this dish, but the Puy lentil, originating from the south of France, is regarded as the king of lentils. Puy lentils have a superior refined flavor and always retain their shape and texture.

• Preheat the oven to 350°F/180°C. Press the cloves into the onion. Put the lentils into a large casserole, then add the onion and bay leaf and pour in the stock. Cover and cook in the preheated oven for 1 hour.
• Remove the onion and discard the cloves. Slice the onion and return it to the casserole with the vegetables. Stir thoroughly and season to taste with salt and pepper. Cover and return to the oven for 1 hour.
• Discard the bay leaf. Stir in the lemon juice and serve straight from the casserole.

SERVES 4

¼ cup sun-dried tomatoes, chopped
1⅛ cups Puy lentils
2½ cups cold water
2 tbsp olive oil
½–1 tsp crushed dried chilies
2–3 garlic cloves, chopped
1 large onion, cut into small wedges
1 small celery root, cut into small chunks
8 oz/225 g carrots, sliced
8 oz/225 g new potatoes, scrubbed and cut into chunks
1 small acorn squash, seeded, peeled, and cut into small chunks, about 8 oz/225 g prepared weight
2 tbsp tomato paste
1¼ cups vegetable stock
1–2 tsp hot paprika
few fresh sprigs of thyme
1 lb/450 g ripe tomatoes

TO SERVE
sour cream
crusty bread

Vegetable Goulash

If the squash is not available, you could use the same quantity of sweet potatoes or parsnips, cut into small chunks.

• Put the sun-dried tomatoes in a small heatproof bowl, then cover with almost boiling water and let soak for 15–20 minutes. Drain, reserving the soaking liquid. Meanwhile, rinse and drain the lentils, then put them in a pan with the cold water and bring to a boil. Reduce the heat, then cover and simmer for 15 minutes. Drain and set aside.

• Heat the oil in a large, heavy-bottom pan, with a tight-fitting lid, and cook the chilies, garlic, and vegetables, stirring frequently, for 5–8 minutes, or until softened. Blend the tomato paste with a little of the stock in a pitcher and pour over the vegetable mixture, then add the remaining stock, lentils, the sun-dried tomatoes and their soaking liquid, and the paprika and thyme.

• Bring to a boil, then reduce the heat and simmer, covered, for 15 minutes. Add the fresh tomatoes and simmer for an additional 15 minutes, or until the vegetables and lentils are tender. Serve topped with spoonfuls of sour cream, accompanied by crusty bread.

SERVES 4

1 red onion
2 tbsp olive oil
2–4 garlic cloves, crushed
1 fresh red chili, seeded and sliced
1 eggplant, about 8 oz/ 225 g, cut into small chunks
small piece fresh gingerroot, peeled and grated
1 tsp ground cumin
1 tsp ground coriander
pinch of saffron threads or ½ tsp turmeric
1–2 cinnamon sticks
½–1 butternut squash, about 1 lb/450 g, peeled, seeded and cut into small chunks
8 oz/225 g sweet potatoes, cut into small chunks
scant ½ cup no-soak prunes
scant 2–2½ cups vegetable stock
4 tomatoes, chopped
14 oz/400 g canned chickpeas, drained and rinsed
1 tbsp chopped fresh cilantro, to garnish

Moroccan Hot Pot

If you like, sprinkle over some chopped no-soak dried apricots or the seeds from a pomegranate before serving. Freshly prepared couscous or bulgur wheat would be ideal to serve with this stew.

- Finely chop the onion. Heat the oil in a large, heavy-bottom pan with a tight-fitting lid, and cook the onion, garlic, chili, and eggplant, stirring frequently, for 5–8 minutes, or until softened.
- Add the ginger, cumin, ground coriander, and saffron and cook, stirring constantly, for 2 minutes. Bruise the cinnamon stick.
- Add the cinnamon, squash, sweet potatoes, prunes, stock, and tomatoes to the pan and bring to a boil. Reduce the heat, then cover and simmer, stirring occasionally, for 20 minutes.
- Add the chickpeas to the pan and cook for an additional 10 minutes. Discard the cinnamon and serve garnished with the fresh cilantro.

Index